T0197593

MIDNIGHT SAILOR

Written & Illustrated by:
Sharon Balardo

AuthorHouse™
1663 Liberty Drive
Bloomington, IN 47403
www.authorhouse.com
Phone: 833-262-8899

Because of the dynamic nature of the Internet, any web addresses or links contained in this book may have changed
since publication and may no longer be valid. The views expressed in this work are solely those of the author and do not
necessarily reflect the views of the publisher, and the publisher hereby disclaims any responsibility for them.

Any people depicted in stock imagery provided by Getty Images are models,
and such images are being used for illustrative purposes only.
Certain stock imagery © Getty Images.

This book is printed on acid-free paper.

ISBN: 978-1-4490-9611-3 (sc)

Library of Congress Control Number: 2010903204

Print information available on the last page.

Published by AuthorHouse

Rev. Date: 11/21/2021

authorHOUSE®

Dedicated to my children
Greg, Tim, and Katie
Who, with an abundance of
Patience and perseverance,
Completed their own journeys of
"Midnight Sailing".

Love Mom

MIDNIGHT SAILOR

Sam had sailboats on his undershirts

He had sailboats on his socks

As soon as Sam was old enough

He'd venture to the docks.

Sammy was born to sail...

He always dressed in sailor suits

Made by the finest tailor

Sam was still too young to sail a ship

But he was a constant midnight sailor.

Sammy was born to sail...

**Midnight Sailor – Colloquialism for bed wetter

A midnight sailor

At age five and six

Oh how Sammy wished

He could find a fix.

Sammy was born to sail...

"Patience young Sam,"

His father would state.

"You could be a midnight sailor

At age seven or eight."

Sammy was born to sail...

Sammy searched desperately

To find the source

But midnight sailing

Took its natural course.

Sammy was born to sail...

"Patience young Sam,"

His father stated again.

"You could be a midnight sailor

At age nine or ten."

Sammy was born to sail...

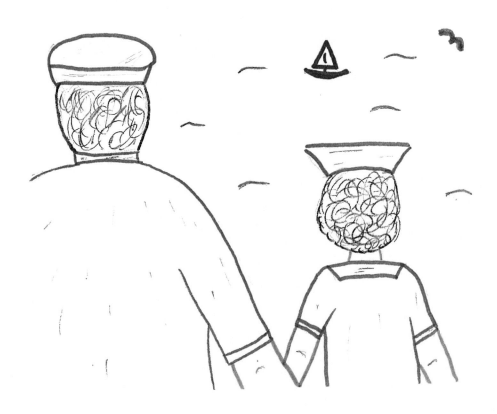

Discouraged was Sammy

His frustration grew

But he would believe his father

This he knew.

Sammy was born to sail...

As Sammy grew taller

And his suit grew tight

He completed his journey

Of sailing at night.

Sammy was born to sail…

A midnight sailor

Until age eleven

Completing this journey

Seemed like a gift from heaven!

Sammy was born to sail...

Sammy shouted to his father

A captain of the sea,

"No more midnight sailing!"

"Yes son, you were just like me."

Sammy was born to sail...

Sammy's eyes grew wide

He couldn't believe his ears,

"You were a midnight sailor

For years and years?"

Sammy was born to sail...

"Not just me son

And not just you

There's been many a midnight sailor

If you only knew."

Sammy was born to sail...

Patience the secret

Mother Nature did not fail

Captain Sammy of the SS Lit

Replaced the midnight sail.

Sammy was born to sail!

**Lit - Pronounced "Lee" - French word meaning bed

A NOTE TO ALL PARENTS

Should bed wetting be an issue in your family,
Welcome it with open arms and say, "Thank you."
There is so much more out there that
"Mother Nature" cannot fix.

ABOUT THE AUTHOR

Author Sharon Balardo writes her therapeutic children's book from her heart and from her own experiences as a mother raising her three children who were each faced with the challenge of bed wetting. In the Balardo household, bed wetting was referred to as midnight sailing, a good natured way to refer to a challenge that would eventually be outgrown by all three children. As Sharon Balardo completed her teacher certification at D'Youville College in 2007/2008, she was required to write two children's books as course assignments. Writing from the heart, Sharon mentally wrote the bulk of Midnight Sailor one evening as she was driving home from D'Youville College, Buffalo, New York to Hamilton, Ontario, Canada. Sharon Balardo regards herself as parent first, teacher/author second. She leaves her reader with this thought to ponder. "There are many challenges in the world and actually very few problems. The difference between the two is that challenges can be fixed, in time, whereas problems cannot. Indeed bed wetting is simply a challenge that most children outgrow. If bed wetting is an issue in your family, welcome it with open arms because there are other "problems" that mother nature cannot fix."

Printed in the United States
by Baker & Taylor Publisher Services